AINBOW LEGENDS ALPHABET

EQUAL RIGHTS

Words by Robin Feiner

A is for **A**nderson Cooper. This influential journalist, author and news anchor became the first openly gay person to moderate an official presidential debate. Cooper, who believes "being gay is a blessing," was honored with the Vito Russo Award by the gay rights organization, GLAAD.

B is for **B**arbara Gittings. What do we owe Barbara? Everything. As the 'mother of the LGBT civil rights movement,' she was a tireless activist who fought against censorship and discrimination for the gay community. "Equal treatment – no more, no less" was her mantra.

C is for Laverne Cox. Beautiful inside and out, Laverne is a shining light for those who struggle to be accepted. The first openly transgender person to win an Emmy, she is a fearless trailblazer in her advocacy for gender acceptance and equality.

D is for Stormé **D**eLarverie. Remembered as a gay civil rights icon, it's said that her scuffle with police sparked the legendary Stonewall Riots. She was an entertainer, nightclub bouncer and gay superhero who voluntarily patrolled the streets to protect her fellow lesbians.

E is for **E**llen DeGeneres. She shook the world when she came out to Oprah and then did it again when her sitcom character did the same. They canceled her show, but you can't keep a legend down for long. More than four million people tune in to 'Ellen' every day.

Ff

F is for Barney **F**rank. This legend of U.S. politics campaigned for equality throughout a long and distinguished career. His open and unashamedly gay political agenda included the right to marry, the right to serve in the military and the right to employment based on qualifications, not sexual orientation.

G is for **G**ilbert Baker. This artist and political activist helped define the modern LGBTQI movement by designing the rainbow flag. The eight vibrant colors represent sex, life, healing, sunlight, nature, art, serenity and spirit. Most importantly, the colors represent the diversity of the community.

Hh

H is for **H**arvey Milk.
One of the first openly gay people elected to public office, Harvey believed that community promoted unity and was the key to better lives for LGBTQI people. His activism for human rights, environment, labor and neighborhood issues earned him legendary status.

I is for Ian McKellen. Admired for his depth of character and legendary sense of humor, Sir Ian has won every major theatrical award in the U.K. He has also been nominated for Academy Awards and Emmys. But he puts just as much heart into his championing of LGBTQI social justice movements worldwide.

J is for Elton John.
One of the world's best-loved musicians, the 'Rocket Man,' Sir Elton John, was among the first to join the fight against HIV/AIDS.
His passion and personal generosity ensure that his foundation continues to raise valuable funds for research and support programs.

K is for **K**eith Haring. This pop art legend became famous for his quirky chalk outline drawings in New York's subways. He used his talent to raise awareness of gay issues, and through his art, his foundation continues to support children's charities and AIDS organizations.

L is for **L**ady Gaga.
Singer, songwriter, actress and style icon, this bisexual lady is a passionate and vocal role model. Her legendary song 'Born This Way' has become an anthem for the struggle for acceptance in the LGBTQI community, and her foundation actively supports equality causes worldwide.

Mm

M is for Martina Navratilova. One of the greatest tennis players the game has ever seen – winning 18 singles Grand Slams – Navratilova led the way for others as an openly gay professional athlete in the 1980s. For her ongoing support for gay rights groups, she was awarded the National Equality Award.

N is for Neil Patrick Harris. This talented actor, writer, comedian, magician and singer was the first openly gay person given the honor of hosting the Academy Awards. Along with husband David and their twins, his happy rainbow family is famous for its legendary Halloween costumes.

O is for Rosie O'Donnell. Mom of five, Rosie has long been an outspoken advocate for lesbian rights, gay adoption and foster care issues. As a comedian, actress, author, producer and talk show host, she is famous for never backing down from her beliefs.

P is for Ru**P**aul.
Diva, actor, model, singer
and queer pioneer, he was
the first-ever drag queen
to become a national talk
show host. His award-winning
creation 'RuPaul's Drag Race'
proudly sashays the art of
drag down the runway and
into living rooms across
the world.

Q is for 'Queer Eye's' Fab Five. Improving the world one straight guy at a time, the original 'Fab Five' burst into our living rooms in 2003. Their sharp sense of style, quick wit and general adorableness quickly endeared audiences and helped the LGBTQI community take ownership and pride in the word 'queer.'

R is for Bayard **R**ustin. He organized Freedom Rides to end racial discrimination and advised Martin Luther King Jr. on non-violent strategies that improved the lives of African Americans. Rustin came to believe that gay rights were the new barometer for social change.

S is for Michael Sam.
The first publicly gay player
to be drafted to the NFL,
Michael was congratulated
by President Barack Obama
for his bravery. In 2014,
Missouri students formed a
human wall to block anti-gay
protesters at a ceremony
in his team's honor.

T is for **T**im Cook.
At the pinnacle of success,
Cook is the CEO of tech giant,
Apple and the first openly
gay person on the Fortune
500 list. His vision and
determination is legendary,
and he applies it to his belief
that "we pave the sunlit
path toward justice together,
brick by brick."

U is for Karl Heinrich **Ulrichs.**
This lawyer, journalist and
author was a true pioneer.
In 1867, Karl delivered a
speech denouncing anti-
gay laws, one of the first
ever public defenses of
homosexuality. Reflecting
on his life, he wrote that
"until my dying day I will
look back with pride that
I found the courage."

Vv

**V is for Gianni Versace.
This flamboyant Italian fashion
designer had a "brazen defiance
of the rules of fashion." He
and long-time partner Antonio
counted royalty and rock stars
as friends. Gianni is survived
by his sister Donatella, who
is now proudly a Stonewall
Ambassador and gay icon.**

Ww

W is for Edith **W**indsor. This strong-willed pioneer fought for marriage equality, and it is because of her that laws were changed to extend equal rights to same-sex couples. As a technology forerunner, Windsor helped LGBTQI groups become tech literate, build databases and communicate more effectively.

Xx

X is for Cynthia Nixon. Famous for her role as Miranda on the TV show 'Sex and the City,' this award-winning actress is a longtime advocate for same-sex marriage and LGBTQI rights. She married in 2012, saying, "I'm just a woman in love with another woman." In 2018, she revealed that her oldest child is transgender.

Y is for Yves Saint Laurent. At only 21 years of age, he became head designer for Dior. But it was in creating his own label and revered fashion house that he revolutionized ready-to-wear fashion. Days before his death, he joined in a same-sex civil union with long-term partner, Pierre Bergé. To this day, their estate contributes to AIDS research.

Z is for **Z**achary Quinto. As a popular actor and gay rights activist, Quinto is passionately active in the area of suicide prevention among LGBTQI youth. He supports the 'It Gets Better' project, giving hope to those who are struggling to be accepted or to accept themselves. What a legend.

The ever-expanding legendary library

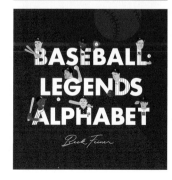

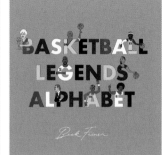

EXPLORE THESE LEGENDARY ALPHABETS & MORE AT WWW.ALPHABETLEGENDS.COM

RAINBOW LEGENDS ALPHABET
www.alphabetlegends.com

Published by Alphabet Legends Pty Ltd in 2019
Created by Beck Feiner
Copyright © Alphabet Legends Pty Ltd 2019

UNICEF AUSTRALIA
A portion of the Net Proceeds from the sale of this book
are donated to UNICEF.

9780648506386